A Castle in Spain

Daniel Neumann

A Castle in Spain

Acknowledgements

Some of these poems were first published in *The Sydney Morning Herald*, *Meanjin*, *Overland*, *Quadrant*, *The Canberra Times*, *Friendly Street Reader* No. 9, *Antipodes* (USA), 'Let Dark Memory Bloom' (Newcastle Poetry Competition 1995), and 'Hand Luggage Only' (Online Sonnet Competition 2007–8).

A Castle in Spain
ISBN 978 1 76041 486 3
Copyright © text Daniel Neumann 2018

First published 2018 by
GINNINDERRA PRESS
PO Box 3461 Port Adelaide 5015 Australia
www.ginninderrapress.com.au

Contents

Three-Thirty	7
Top Paddocks	8
Life Cycle	9
Rockabye Baby	10
Ex-husband	11
Trammie	12
Auslit 101	13
Attila	14
Studies on Hysteria	15
To a Friend, Exchanging Copies of *The Three Fates*	18
Clara's Friend	19
Mozart in Australia	20
A View of Two Theatres	22
Sunday at Geoff's	23
Mathematician in the English Class	24
Scenes From a Life	26
A Work of Art	29
Lunch Stop (Boggabilla)	30
Introductions, Brandy Marys	32
Entering Middle Age in Carlton	34
The Invitation	36
Clearing	37
Four Sydney Postcards	38
Coach Comes Home	41
Agent to Artist	42
Building a Railway Off the Tablelands	44
Dr Freud	45
Country Funeral	46
Haiku: A History of Western Thought	48
Good Friday	49

Two Moments	50
The Orchestra Plays Canberra	51
Riddle	52
The Beginning	54
Haiku: Sibelius	57
Two Poems From *The Guide to Greece* (2nd century AD)	58
A Castle in Spain	60
The Recital	62
The New Kenyans	64
Mrs Nemeth	67
Under the Volcano	68
Going to Visit the Grave	70
The Granite Poem	71
Notes	73

Three-Thirty

One night I dreamt enormous bubbles
grew in the asphalt schoolyard.
Something to hatch, I thought, and here
at last it comes:
a sturdy mistress of monkey bars
and off-ground tiggy swings on the frame
three rungs at a time or shins up a pole
to traverse a six-foot bar… I tried
that too, and the principal crossing the yard:
'What else can she do that you can't do?'
Plenty. And her sister can dance like a leaf –
two children airborne, ladder-bright
while dad works out on a pillow of stones.

Top Paddocks

Our family's not the sort to settle down
same place we've been brought up. Liking the slope of this
I got it with the money when mum died;
and never married. Though, I could have once –
she had a body to her like these hills,
if they stood up they'd be tall like her. See how
they curve like tits to a belly, grazing the stock.
She's withered, I hear (well, I have too: the ills
the flesh is heir to) but I never went to see.
There's not been time with having a place of my own
and labour's dear; it's hard work now
not like the old days. Besides
men remember where married women forget.
I wrote, of course, years back: she never replied.

Life Cycle

There are three well-known chapters. First, the young
pushing of city limits, the coastal creep,
a clearing of trees or a miner's exploration.
Next the glamorous, well and frequently sung
proof and dance of courage, the gay brave leap:
a desert trek, a world circumnavigation.
And after this decisive act has sprung
from a trigger of books or a woman who looks deep
into the privacies of imagination
and new unheard-of bounds are set among
the certainties which maps and tables keep,
horizons cease to represent vocation
and settlement begins: a generation
of colonial cities, children, broken sleep.

Rockabye Baby

From America I heard
this tale of an average boy
threw such a mental, truly
nothing doctors could do
but hang *psychotic* on him.

His parents sent him away
to an uncle on the land.
First thing on arrival
young nutcase finds a tree,
climbs forty feet off the ground.

He stayed up there three days
all weathers and wouldn't come down;
was cured when he did. You wouldn't
read about it, said doctors
one or two sharpening chainsaws.

Ex-husband

He understood at last, he'd never come
from Jacob's wrestling visionary seed;
and his desire to be that way was some
accident, whose cause there was no need
to chase up alleys. Turn, they told him, look:
your personal angel is no night-long foe –
more of a casual tutor, hands a book,
pointing a passage you might like to know:
a topic for discussion, or a code
of conduct for a husband and a father.
He brings existence in an easier mode,
the lying tongues went on: for sure you'd rather
buy soft books and soft drinks on the train
than grapple with an angel in the plain?

Of course the break-up hurt. He kept the pain
to make a shrivelled sinew for his thigh.

Trammie

Knock-off time? let's hope –
sucks a tube of Invalid Stout
up the hill near the roundabout
(looks Valid to me). 19, 18
he lets go, staring townwards, eyeing off
distance in the lunch-hour sun,
drover-fashion…must march to a different tram,
Maribyrnong perhaps? His neat
uniformed arm makes the slow ancient
off-duty salute, he swallows

and on the seat
eleven more invalids wait their turn.

Auslit 101

Austpoetry was a continent pioneered
by the Seven Larger Than Life. They cleared,
subdivided, put the trochees up
– of course, we'd have achieved that
but once the land's settled
may as well spend your days on the beach

make hip-hollows, adjust your pitch
among thousands sensible of the tide
and angle of the sun

The holdings inland
let the companies run.

Attila

He cut off the sleeve
put the shirt in the drawer
days later knelt by the track
thrust his right arm under
but the train took him as well.

Fourteen, he'd lain across
right across, but the afternoon
was suddenly trainless.
Further up he learnt
the goods had killed already.

So death like his mother
left him on his own.
He spent for years *I'm happy*
My love sews by my side
We listen to an old freight train pass

Meeting the instalments
he heard his arm was interest
went looking to pay but
met repossession.

Trains echo through his verse.

Studies on Hysteria

(Freud/Breuer)

It was a well-known theme, retold
in rhythms appropriate for the age –
a quest for kingship, with the old
first labour: free a woman's hand
from chains of monster's silent rage.

All the ingredients were there:
your labyrinth, your crooked thread,
your older man who did not dare
go twice beyond the entrance, and
the younger chose to go instead –

so through the corridors of mind
both radial and peripheral,
and ever-dark, he went to find
the foe; and learnt to understand
the bricked-up doorways in the wall

that took his notice by the way,
and minor characters who came
like ragged princes in a play
hiding their birth as contraband –
these and much more: he learnt to tame

the beast itself; so then he grew
adventurous, heroic, wise,
philosopher and agent who
discovered in himself the land
appropriate to his enterprise.

All that of course came later. Here
we see him finding out his own
power – but with what strength and clear
strategy, as if he planned
a life's attack already known.

So Theseus chose to sail for Crete
undoubtedly because he knew
much of what he was to meet;
and being born into a grand
line and time of heroes, slew

with courage, speed and certainty.
In Athens, tribute-free, now lives
his everyday posterity
– that's us: the miles and years are spanned
by what the common hero gives.

And what of Breuer, the friend who had
himself the key and half the maps?
– I find his figure rather sad.
He feared the personal demand
implicit in their work, perhaps;

or was too scrupulous to bring
his patient's sudden loving craze
into the therapeutic ring –
all one. The monster's turn and stand
drove him forever from the maze.

To a Friend, Exchanging Copies of *The Three Fates**

This game we share as livelihood
persuading chancy hair and wood
to move exactly as they should

takes lifetimes learning. Sure, we know
the music must direct the bow
and all the hand need do is follow

but easier said than done! there'll be
long year before it happens. We
learn from exemplars, though, agree

that here's one in her craft; so I'm
glad to exchange with this poor rhyme
our gifts of Rosemary and time.

* by Rosemary Dobson

Clara's Friend

'In the dream I stopped & got out,
went & pushed on the bonnet – like
I was trying to get control?'
                        We nod
and sip our tea at the wide table
in a sunny jumble of books. She brushes
hair tentatively away from her face
but she'd dealt with the car, knew it'd never
catch fire again.
                Later, softly
unwinds about a relationship;
came dressed in overalls this afternoon
as if restoring a garage of difficult cars.

Mozart in Australia

(i) Rehearsal

There's a small road in this sudden change
to relative minor: lies through a sweep
of purple, disappears over the range
somewhere near Albury. A deep
profusion of flowering weeds, cloud-shadows, grass
brushed by hand across the hills;
the road climbs dustily towards a pass,
turns at the saddle a moment, spills
softly down across a patch of sorrow's
coolness… But Marcellina's found her son
behind desk three of fiddles; Figaro's
delighted, so's Susanna; my lord's fun
baulked again: he's ropeable – though soon…

Small children of a landscape, they traverse
its intricate ancient slopes this afternoon
through Spain, through Salzburg, rich in Paterson's curse.

(ii) Fiordiligi

Her country can still show a heartbreak smile
of grace, though now its rivers run
inland – fidelity and pride
used up far from the sea. Meanwhile
no worries in the audience, they make fun
and so does he; weeps by her side
though too, like rain. The arias shape
grace to a passionate half-escape

before defeat. You've seen the Wimmera? miles
and miles it nourishes a fringe
of stately trees; but then the sun
beats rivers down. Alfonso smiles
to see the officers strut, the ladies cringe,
his hundred guineas neatly won –
what could survive in such dry air?
– yet leaves them in a country where

desert is missing. Sure, the map
shows no great rivers on this plain
she's reached; but things will grow. They tap
groundwater, and here's frequent rain.

A View of Two Theatres

The hydrofoils curved out and back
swishing their wake like long hair. Half a year
south we sidestep drunken Jack;

no ferries now but waterless views
from an exercise yard for trees. Power poles
wait around like cold-faced screws.

Winter leaches the last deposits
of harboured summer. Time to leave,
across the traffic – but in the sandpit

kneeling, *I'll build a tower*, quick hand
to push the hair from her eyes. Absorbed
she digs deep where the thing will stand

leaving the tower for superstructure.
A long way down below ground level
is where it happens; the new theatre's

no promontory launched at the sun,
no white flames swept from glittering sea
and caught there (shows may also run)

– nothing flamboyant like that, this town.
But deep around her envisaged act
she hollows a cave one afternoon

and later, quietly, the spare
material's shaped into the air.

Sunday at Geoff's

Halfway through the job on Barry's Ford
we broke for lunch. Geoff brought the gearbox
mainshaft in and dropped it on the table
victorious: My style is groaning board

but got the old *Ah Geoffrey* from Lorraine
with back-up vocals. *Put it on the floor,
there's newspaper* and never a break
discussing family in Castlemaine

with all it brings to mind, like Melanie bought
that house up Heathcote way? Barb's graduated?
the news gets handed round the table
with cabanossi; Petra Hackney's caught

creative like a disease… Well Geoff's been touched
with that, I said. He'd gone out back to watch
his natives grow, the old house settle down
with friends on board. We've heard he writes, not much,

just needs to step outside. Geoff's pretty stable
but a man can't spend his whole life round a table.

Mathematician in the English Class

('I'll put a Gödel round about the earth / In forty minutes!')

In a late tutorial, vexed
by the tick of the four-o'clock
interpreters of the text,
he dreamed of the wide-arm shock
If they'd only give us a key!
– not these algorithms to prove
computable things to be true,
but instructions for putting to sea
from a traveller drunk with love,
and the rest could be up to you

– though imperfectly aware
that the sea is a universe,
and gulping black holes there
could incontinently reverse
the shape of fallers-in
Some distant corner of space
you might reappear, if at all,
with your feet sticking out of your face
and a transcendental grin
on your lower abdominal wall

and more – the simple, yet
the great entropic touch
Time has no finite set
of transformations such
as these, to bring you through
– encircling time – to where
you found yourself before
No footsteps passed the door
but others felt a chair
turn void, unproveably true.

Scenes From a Life

When – many years after he disappeared –
you go in search of Uncle W
ask first at Bertrand Russell House
where his family were wardens.
He's not one they acknowledge
easily, his mum saying, 'We sent him
on all the school excursions, I must confess
with too little money. He would have bought
nothing but biscuits,' and Dad:
'I got him riding-clothes at his own
insistence (with my approval; he was always correct)
but I never heard of him anywhere near a horse,'
while on the block behind the college
he peopled the weeds with stories of the gods.

Aeaea entranced him (much to the amusement
of Circe's friends at PLC)
– the island curved round him on his arrival there
rising inland a crescent of blossoming trees,
crystals of summer. For the first time he knew
himself Odysseus, treading the latent glory
of his wandering.

                       The goddess couldn't keep him
long – he had Penelope to think about
and besides the sailors came ashore on his tracks
rasping for whores. No wonder
he carried a crew of pigs for so many years!
He worked his teaching bond in country towns
looked knowledgeably at horses (but they bite)
wolfed biscuits when no one was looking
and played at trains on the buckled rails
of Aquinas Siding with rusticated priests.
Dusty as they were they drew morals for him
e.g. the metals
are kept exactly apart by imprecise
ties of homely timber, never meet
bar infinity 'which we have other names for'
– he'd stand for hours staring at the vanishing point.

Then details fade. A fragment shows
he took the tin hare to an inland railhead
(of next year's kids most had his nose)
hitchhiked towards the centre, sleeping
in wreckers' yards...

                Yeah, somebody called that
was a bit of a legend out there.
Some put him behind
half the swy in Alice; others said
Stylites of the Coolibahs, His Grace
last seen up a tree, raving, blind
and a parcel of tame crows spotting out the land.

A Work of Art

(after the drawing by William Delafield Cook, in the Queensland Art Gallery, Brisbane)

Why yes, it is a matter for tears, Miranda –
the bird in a glass bowl cowering under
a gesture, and the magus daring us all
with his fine sharpness and ravening talent –
but do be reasonable. This is a work of art.
Look, the critics are discussing it already,
the imprisonment will be forgotten soon;
besides, Father would like us to be proud.
Come, sister, stand by me at the window,
use the night framed with such effect – the moon,
the clouds racing to their decease, with no
other habitation near… Consider,
and calm yourself before you face the crowd:
the gallery for whom this work was done.

Lunch Stop (Boggabilla)

Twenty-two-wheelers
like club singers
howling past a mike
appear from nowhere
   before they're introduced
   get silence down and stomp it
turn your back to them
they're gone already

Roadhouse and railhead
the permanents
scrape each other's bones
under the cross-rhythm
   – I'm how it's done in Marrickville
     and round here from now on
   – I could carry all yours to Central yet
     always have done
Neither troubles
to mend fences

The ticket window
closed like a cupboard
The rails still half-awake
three hundred miles
of worn stitching
end in the grass
The two signals
dry and distant
  – you may/you may not
like curates in a field
  – Ah, but safe working
  is good scripture

Across the road
smooth as sunglasses
our alloy capsule
waits on gravel
  – by the food trough for cowboys
  random as chaos, grumbles a local
  – says a layout run to last year's timetable
  by grown men in a playground, sneers the other
as we gather back on time to a runway
of dead grevilleas, our driver cool in shorts
adjusting mirrors for the next session of history

clamber up
now tea bags have done their worst
roll out to boogie
past other mikes

Introductions, Brandy Marys

There's no pub at Brandy Marys,
how could there be? the valley's drowned.
Scraping like bark ghosts in the wind
the men wear out their old stories:

> 'I was sent here as a geologist.
> Sank too many for their liking,
> took core samples y wouldn't credit
> and neither did they. Talking of credit
> this is Mary, she'll take y cheque…
> Y find caverns here, unbelievable
> the crystals, the formations
> – I couldn't bring 'em up.'

> 'That bloke with the fishing eyes
> and all the marks of excellent tackle
> (which he had, till an incident)
> – known as Murray Codpiece.
> Sort of desert father twice removed
> once from fatherhood and once to this,
> won't remove again. Thanks Mary.'

> 'Jock inhabits the morose side of the hill.
> Trout fisherman, used to run
> sheep on the high country
> – fed his sheep on the trout, we reckon,
> never brought any down here.
> Spends all his time now selling us wool.'

'He's got no wool;
and meet Solomon, one-string fiddle.
Made when they used good timber,
lovely finish, knew their work
but Sol come here tight as a nuns.
Mary reached in, pulled his sound post over,
now he sings at a touch
– all of four notes.'

There's no pub at Brandy Marys,
never was but in the mind
where later mighty dams have drowned
her trade with all their histories.

Entering Middle Age in Carlton

Our lazy conversations treat
of shoes and yachts, bikini wax,
the running speed of Shadowfax,
Paul Simon's early songs. We greet
the audience from a thighbone seat
of outdoor chairs on Lygon Street.

The pastel shops will soon delete
the way we knew it once, but Slacks
can still remember all the facts
to tell White Jeans *The butcher beat
his wife with slabs of flyblown meat
and sold them too, down Lygon Street.*

The afternoon's a warm conceit
of everything that wisdom lacks –
the kitsch, the new, the blister packs
of rainbow condoms fit to eat
or velvet larks with wired-on feet
who sing for cash in Lygon Street,

while twenty-five-year-olds with fleet
Mercedes-Benzes claimed off tax
go by in shirts like coloured sacks;
they've made a mint, they live on neat
champagne; how wildly they compete
for parking space on Lygon Street!

Full speed, the engine-noise is sweet.
But in the darkness something cracks
two miles away. The lookout quacks
Ice dead ahead!
               – *Thank you*; complete
professionals, of course, we'll meet
our moonlit bergs off Lygon Street

in time, no doubt; but in this heat
who can believe it? With long blacks
curled in our hands, we leave no tracks;
read book reviews and live discreet
unpublished brilliant tales, replete
with all our years on Lygon Street.

The Invitation

How do you deal with unwelcome callers? the sort
like those who yearly bring to my door a plain
old-fashioned hip bath filled with (they say) water?
I put them off politely, fearing pain
– for no, that isn't from taps, it's an oily rich
corrosive. I imagine that on skin
like paint stripper or caustic soda, which
we're careless with from time to time.
                                                    Get in?
be stung and eaten raw, blood flesh dissolving
till they take me out and rinse the skeleton clean
as grinning driftwood, a xylophone to play
tunes round the city? *Not now*, I usually say,
Perhaps next year if I'm not too busy… I mean
colouring children's eggs, that sort of thing.

Clearing

(a painting by Rod McCrae)

Now one by one the flames move off,
tall nodding bands of ochre light.
Within their hurricane's soft eye
slow nimbus gathers to a face
unhardened yet; and at its core
is glowing cloud or molten rock,
whose fingers shape themselves from fire.

Four Sydney Postcards

(i) Rock Carvings, Kuringai

The small plants rustle when you brush past
Any time you can bend or shake a tree
Bare rock is quiet, all weathers.

On a country clothed in whispering children
creased by rain and wind
these hard scrapes of oldness
Other children come to them

A meeting for all of us
Like small rain and wind
carve our pattern on his bones

(ii) Lines on a Bronze Bust*

Within a circular Bed of bright
Ranunculus, there blooms waist-height
A small inverted Plinth. On this,
Green *Arthur Phillip* squats amiss
– Mere Head and Shoulders. Some Surprise
Informs the mighty Governor's Eyes
(His Limbs encas'd by Earthy Powers)
At being arrested thus, with Flowers.

---

* near the old Maritime Services Board building

(iii) Macquarie Place

The guys unwound on summer evenings
beneath those trees. Superb in tailored shorts
we grappled characters two foot high – the kings,
the queens and bishops, bowled about their courts
by officers crisp and mighty in a land
of knee-high tokens. All gone home, to play
unshapely middle games. Some planner's hand
revoked the board or one too many stray
white rook cost half the till. Now walls of glass
compete for the remaining sun; we heard
their clamour from foundation, let it pass
to check the moves or a likely-looking bird,
or shout (the pub's gone too); and at the Quay
their shadows touch the navigable sea.

(iv) Last of Their Kind

Leans on a patch of wall
outside the chemist
scuffs the arcade floor
sleeps here all night
on the mosaic

Or hunched under a stairwell
slowly coughs when you give
20c gets yer to Homebush, pal
don't waste it
more won't go farther

Red Phones with smokers' breath
ex-jovial round-shouldered jockeys
are losing their turf
can't make the long distances
– never could
Some crouch in old booths,
pretend they still can.

Coach Comes Home

He used the long walk to 'Dunromin'
as fielding practice. She'd have heard
of course, and though the brief two-word
    affair was closed, you're never sure with women.

Been great, fuck off, the girl had said
– the thanks he got, a real disgrace!
and people near them knew his face
    so, tales get told. He stumbled, rubbed his head:

It's been a puzzle how to bat.
Straight down the pitch and keep it nice
like Dad, with leg byes once or twice
    when they were offered? No great score, but that

kept sweet; or slam around the wicket
like old times? But old times recalled
in-swingers (in his mind, no-balled)
    like this, who'd found his gaps and spoilt the cricket.

Agent to Artist

Keep you thin do I?
Listen
When you're lean
I can be your fat man. Every thin man
gotta have a fat man, & I'm yours.
You come to me for towels and tobacco
stamps & that
I'll pay the gym fees
& where the money come from?

Listen
Crowds bring it
I shape the crowd, see
I make the ring
You gotta have a ring, lean man
Gotta bounce off the ropes
gotta break to the corners
When you're thin you know where they are
& my bein fat?
Listen

You know crowds
I gotta wear flesh
When they see a thin man make his own ring
they say *Ain't no show*
& look away
When they see thin men puttin on weight
they spit & depart
When they see a fat man
they say *He's eating*
His thin men are good
& spend the housekeeping

That's the gamble, thin man
I don't say they'll always
& when they don't you'll be through thin
out the other side
but you keep goin
& I'll stay swell
that's always been
how thin men sell

Building a Railway Off the Tablelands

It felt as if we'd never reach the coast:
good engines scrapped for parts, the missing coal,
the ceaseless damp corruption. Where's our boast
of always muddling through? And then the goal
was shifting on the quiet behind our backs:
Surprise! we heard, The dry red heart's the place
– and nobody but nobody lays tracks:
down tools, and go on foot. Which, with bad grace
or thoughtless glee or what, most of the men did.
Not me; I kept my eyes towards the range
falling sheer into surf, the far-off splendid
engineering still before us. Strange
the way the crowd dissolves from round a man
and turns out right, and he's the also-ran.

Dr Freud

(for my father on his 80th birthday)

A sure physician, though a rigid meta-
physician, upright, sensual; with a touch
of poet in his homely sharpness, much
more in his unshakeable love. Far better
his dry prose all the same; he could deploy
fact and hypothesis but never feint
and pierce with shifting images, nor paint
a world in a quick intensity of joy
– though moved to hear it done. A handicap?
But who like this against the tides of dark
so lit the house with reason? True, like Marx
he left his own humanity off the map
(disastrously for followers – the late
nineteenth century's kept us all confined
in dreams of algorithm); yet with the mind
his only tool he made himself its great
formal cartographer – though left the heart
unmapped, that shaping matrix of his art.

Country Funeral

Death in the last few of that generation
travels a circuit taking seasonals
such as fencing: bends stiff wire together.
At St Peter's we embrace who wouldn't
meet by choice before – better this clutch of mothballs
says the dance – and the shabby
home muster starts with muttered-over cousins
recovering weight as carriers of the genes.

We were such rockets when young, despite
the Notable Sense of Family –
scattered with fizz and flash, touched only
to pull each other's wick in brag of starburst
or disparagement at festive tables
set crosswise to the bridal of the hour.
Forty years not speaking?
– merely an arch of our spectacular
from here to here on the plain, like tracer
visible even by daylight.

                                          Yet fireworks
don't carry as expected, or the ranges
are steadily decamping that we aimed at.
The paddock where the sticks fall
swings overhead already. Secretly
I've started fading colour from my tracks,
learning a new position for landing –
to be glimpsed upside down in shadow
a moment over where our shapers lie,
arms tugged out to both sides of the clan.

Our saintly patron models from his diagram;
meanwhile here's my bone shape, my own gait
stumping across the car park –
heredity on its way to tie me in
for a last three-legged event. Children nursing
egg-and-spoon grandeur or an urge to wrestle
slip through death's mending to carry the carnival
farther out as our stumbling waltz begins.

Haiku: A History of Western Thought

One hundred broke the mirror.
Each holds a fragment
– seven centuries' bad luck

Good Friday

Remember one other year it landed
so late in autumn? Roving the calendar
it scored a battle, that time: the squalls
split off in squadrons line by line
strafing with rain like cannon.
Deep in headquarters
I had the light on, moulding spice and warmth;
the radio shared your gloom about the prospects.

Day after, we had the riverside to ourselves:
the oaks uneasy, fingering cloud
from straggly summer grass and whitish gum,
thin steep grudging paths down the weeds
on a bank being spelled between factories
– but a wealth of acorns, pocketfuls: took them home
to nest with brilliant eggs
and later planted them on open waste.

Otherwise we did little and went nowhere
– not in a mood of curfew, but
touchy with drought and firestorm, glad to use
time down at the gate of winter.
No holidays, the way a carnival road-toll
or chocolate ads would beat the drum for, just
the shift from one to another tilt of axis
confirmed, its orders quietly thumbed like seed.

Two Moments

Not wanting her to leave without a gift
(although in fact they'd never been to bed
or even close, in spite of what was said
by those who knew) he looked at earrings. Thrift
beset him when he saw the price: so tight
with Christmas coming up, and still to get
presents for Margaret and the children – yet
silver and turquoise gleamed against the light
and never would again. She's off to Perth
in seven days, it's a fine job, she'll go
and settle there and marry, never know
unless I give her these. The gesture's worth
a bit of scrape…   Chance meeting, after years:
'Your husband gave me these,' and touched her ears.

The Orchestra Plays Canberra

To winter briefly in a distant half-bowl of
circumspect hills, one afternoon
we drop towards it over its own horizon.
Ranges slide beneath,
long valleys running otherwise whose shoulders
slow down behind, grow tall and lean away
to lodge as background, spilling
thin ends of nightfall.
Taxis scatter like ovens through the dusk,
cold air turns round and bites in hollows.
We come to rest in pockets of empty rooms.

Later the players expand their mornings
shopping or sightseeing round the lake;
regroup for lunch, rehearse
the words for being here: tennis, quartets,
the parliament, such clarity of air! In time
the light declines and mountains burn
from a soft captivity of streets.
The hours draw in towards the start of work.

Eight o'clock is theatre time. Nobody
boxed or galleried here: the crowd
slopes in a tableland
of faces touched with empire, guarding
departmental valleys. Neat ridges of consequence
drain to the landlocked pit. Their pleasure is
Swan Lake, to fill this chamber: so we play
storms off Bass Strait, the turbulence
of all the Southern Ocean; and go home
by star and streetlight, freezing into silence.

Riddle

My first: a filament that thickened
on large-scale maps wherever
two or three thousand were gathered together;
had little to do with the insect dance
of traffic, yet could be seen
often from behind stalled St Christophers;
had many mansions, known to offer sleep
to the poor and homeless; dogmatic against slope
met visible fall with horizontal steel.

Second: in a sixtieth of history
it became the way
fathered out of cities by wilderness:
broad or narrow, formal, colloquial, permanent.
It's still at home between
the odd to each other, valleys of sensual forest
to granite tors of upland chastity;
links both to the towers that radiate urbanity
yet, long before television, had been
the channel: brought word, made news of its own.
Small children watched it. Grown lives went in service.

Last? yes it will, despite the industry
of quick-trip pushers dunning for disuse.
It is one too, hammered daily
in many a town and many a key, but always
second to none the well-known rhythmical
mantra-factory under the mind's floor.

My whole is containment, a travelling door
some enter still for the night journeys of myth
(though more pay less to keep a workday edge
of fingernail courage from blunting on the street);
whose shadow was imperious, undeterred
as *force majeure*, or fate – and still of both
a sometime carriage and common metaphor.

The Beginning

(after the triptych by Max Beckmann in The Met, New York)

Papa was made
by climbing ladders
Mama went with him
as one did
The bearded clown
was left in the cupboard
with orders to come out
if I was wicked

                On the right, teacher
cloned himself from a marble bust
but his shoulders dropped, it didn't work
crucified boys with never a cross
could balance the world on the point of a harp
but never knew, never did; propped the ceiling
with a black girder to stop it falling

And on the left
there was a garlanded girl behind me
always and always turning away
to gaze in her mirror
and I was crowned with spears beside me,
staring in through a black grille
at the organ-grinder winged with angels
and my shield-bearer

So I hung Puss-in-Boots from the light
and leapt on a rocking horse reared to kill
while grandma brought fresh trade each night
to feed my charge, and the clown stayed still

Papa and Mama
cared little for that
They had eyes
for a marble bust
There's your future
my boy, remember
and Mama said Oh!
that woman in green
openly blowing
such bubbles of lust!

But grandma went on reading the paper
the garlanded girl was rapt in her glass
my rocking horse cavalry leapt and capered
– yet sword upraised I could not pass

Stop! cried Papa
gripping the ladder
and Mama said Stop
my dearest child!
reaching between
as well as she could
and they went on climbing
through the room

My rocking horse chilled at the point of its every
topmost leap, and the freezing clown
darkened his mirror, withholding fight
Time and again I armed and rode
on the nursery floor to release them all
for I was born to king and candle
outside the very bars of my crib
not for the world in a classroom, spun
like a globe to the narrow boys looking back
wicked as aren't we over their shoulders

Time and again I creased the floor
and cut a sky of windows out
to sell them off in painted frames
but no one looking where I was
nor ever yet the canvas came
to open round me like a door
and slip a mirror to my hand

Till this beginning, upside down
to start all over without a sword

for Papa and Mama I wept as never
whose ladder finished in my room

could balance the world on the point of a brush
could place my figures before they go
one moment under gallery light
as they were then, as still they are

and ride through cupboards into night.

Haiku: Sibelius

Grips your arm, bruising it –
Look, he says, a lake.
Or walks past, silent. Another lake.

Two Poems From *The Guide to Greece* (2nd century AD)

(i) The Oracle at Lebadeia

I am struck most by the habitat
of divine speech:
not yet wherever two or three are gathered
to hear the Word in upper rooms
but ancient singularities of rock
or cave, or voices in a town –

and mentioned in due order throughout Greece
so that a reader
as if footsore, dusty from the hills,
might find framed with worn tangible stone
of Homer's time, a spring in daily use.

And more: the learned guide himself saying
I have consulted, and seen others do so
offering the water to his friends.

(ii) Lykosoura

Dr Pausanias – rational, devout –
knew much he could have written of Eleusis
but the dream, he said, *forbids me*.

He travelled with an eye for the antiquities,
collating fact with legend. In his book
your scholars see another like themselves

– who now, leaving this temple (noted
for its statue of Demeter and the Mistress
her daughter, whose name may not be told)

returning into the clarity
of Greek light, the air sharp as water

mentions casually a small
mirror set beside the doorway: *Faint
or lacking there, your own reflection, reader
but a clear image of the tall
gods behind you*   throned in sacred quiet
– swift aeons unmoving when you turn the page.

A Castle in Spain

(after Mozart's *Marriage of Figaro*)

Of course you'll agree, there are no permanent gods?
– well yes, I know. But look how each appears
just once in context (though we all take odds
on long repeats): a numen weaving chance
and character into a rigorous knot
demanding – divining – its own resolution, but
mythology straight off. We learn the dance
revealed for a moment out of the passing riot
and relish an intricate lift of heart for years;
but that was then, this now. The god grows quiet.

A knot's to remember. Remember is, carry a braid
from the knot – say woven long ago by a garden
which, one particular summer evening, laid
its revels out and called us into our parts.
Oh we all had lines: the man whose peace and order
came wrapped in ass's skin, the gardener's daughter,
the randy page, the Count, the cuckold hearts
– and each a voice from ordinary life
to speak in arias. When my lord had pardon
last, from a girl in servant clothes (his wife),

the tale despite his arrogance was using him
– and her as well. But then it moved apart,
shedding its players, quietly disabusing them
of weight and pattern. Nobody took harm
or even noticed, drifting up the ride
in costume still, their mischief, love and pride
barely unravelled: a company arm-in-arm.
Two hundred years ago; and never again
though many of us have the act by heart
and thread our lives a different way since then.

Look back. Time grows a country house; we find
a servants' wedding planned; the rest you know.
Its echoes track our long-departed mind
through wars, through franchise (the retreat and distance
are also time). And why beneath those trees
a small fictitious masquerade should blaze
in words and music, edged with such persistence?
That was a knot: a god who wore the face
of time's own children, altering time's flow
with little acts of subterfuge and grace.

The Recital

Frau Kolb would pause and say, He is one of my gods!
– a brief abatement from her task
of crucifying fingers. Ask
for news about him, deprecate the odds

of time and place, of living over here:
it failed each time. She'd met him, live,
but was awake, *natürlich*. Strive
to make as good a sound: play on! Severe

– and optimistic. Yet his legend caught:
a byword for the instrument
even to clods, and we were distant
heirs of his; so I for one have bought

his every disc. Then after twenty years
he came and played at last. Now old,
not much on record – but the hold
such names can have on people! and our ears

could not believe the badness. Yet we stayed,
in taut respect: at interval
took coffee on his phrasing, all
the rest of it; but everyone afraid

of worse to come, and rightly. Halfway through
the last slow movement, in a pause
we heard incongruous applause –
and steadily, appreciative, it grew

a thousand strong. He was after all our friend
so people stood, and there was cheering
even. But he himself, unhearing,
unheard, went on the same way to the end.

The New Kenyans

Before the British came
our people used to call
on wise men's dreams, he said.
They forecast drought, or game,
or battles. Now instead
the white men know it all.

My fathers dreamt: they knew
the times to hunt or sow.
I never dream. A sad
old man bequeaths a few
ironic notes to add
to what the white men know

– recorded just in time
to catch a fading end
of tribal lore. His young
now speak a brother tongue
(cars, wages, urban crime)
to those we comprehend.

But are we further on?
What District Officer took
our dreams? He left his home
in London (earlier, Rome)
to bring us parliaments, look!
But where have our big dreams gone?

So many are small, inane
charades where those we know
behave as they mostly do
(though time is often askew
and place, by a suburb or so)
– form groups, converse, remain,

depart: quotidian Us.
If from the D.O.'s one
or two for whom the brain
is circuitry explain
it's mere debugging, run
in downtime, should we fuss?

They govern for our good:
we neither hunt nor farm,
the cash crop's in plantations,
our weather's understood.
With lucid vaccinations
against all psychic harm

their missions teach our young.
Those great colonial schemes
where profit and duty meld!
– how justly we're compelled
to health and freedom! Dreams
are backward, tribal, wrong.

And yet a shaping lore
survives from long before
this great regime began
its annual Five-year Plan.
Entirely mythic thoughts
have framed our public courts

and still in private, strange
with real-time symptoms (grief,
hope, clarity, distress)
direct to the address
dreams honoured with belief
do bring objective change.

Which I call grace, a name
the dialect has retained.
The D.O. calls it chance:
Oh yes, I saw you dance
but that's not why it rained!
And yet, for all the fame

and credence he enjoys,
his edifice of mind
and world-progressing will
was also once a kind
of soft synaptic noise
time liked. Time chooses still,

and not to his command.
This empire too will call
its governors home, and small
new myths not yet perceived
will grow, join ends: believed,
shape centuries out of hand.

Mrs Nemeth

She had a manager who called her ma'am.
He criticised her shooting, failed to clear
the briar from the paddocks year by year,
and patched the old repairs about the farm.

She dreamed of orchards once. The land was steep
thin fodder in a bowl of air, with rocks
and wire and mortgage. Nights, they heard a fox
he was told off to kill but wouldn't. Sheep

(he left doors open) pastured in the hall –
she'd curse and scuff the droppings out, at least
when people came. At that, he'd vanish. Graced
with cake, she never mentioned him at all.

Still, she was boss. He might be up the end
two miles off, cobbling fences: Charles, she'd say,
hand me that fork. And so throughout the day,
her white hair flowering softly in the wind.

At night she clipped a missing apple tree
or wrote accounts. Accounts of what? he said,
your ancient Europe? Sunday nights they played
at euchre, where he cheated. So did she:

there was no Charles, there never had been. Years
of their companionable life drew in;
she talked to him and heard the silence grin.
The children came for tea and cake: My dears!

There were no children either. When she died
the house was empty and the gate left wide.

Under the Volcano

Turning the lava flow is gamblers' luck,
we knew already. In Hawaii they raided it,
dropping down such a light thread of trajectory
small shapely bombs to tap its crust by fluke
enough askew, and send it tonguing elsewhere.
Some countries fed it houses, or their young.

Off Iceland, nothing we did was tried before.
We climbed on it to quench it. Bulldozer tracks
printing the skin left closing cuts of fire.
With every pump there was
we flung thin freezing jets against
a truck-high crawling cavern of earth's fever.

Magma. This bright awl pierces
thick five-mile slabs of silica, to grow us
our basalt shards in seas of killing cold:
somewhere to stand when playing against the house.

After *be lucky*
the only rule of winning is *be there*.
One of our trawlers fell sideways in winter,
washing its men to chattering death – bar one
seal-thick in fat, we learned, who swam the night out
then walked barefoot across
the razor glass of lava fields, to live.
Now there was luck, and presence!

                                             So.

We had a rock the size of all our houses
come skating slowly to the town.
With plastic wands of sea for fifty hours
we cooled its path and nudged it from our homes
and harbour, keeping our footing on the flow.

Two inches' crust, we found, will hold a man
to play himself between
giants who, red or black, take all

– two inches' luck we still go fishing from.

Going to Visit the Grave

Multas per gentes et multa per aequora vectus…

Despite the formal purpose, he would travel
with feast and dancing; curious to unravel
those ethnic fairy tales and rituals, he
took vivid notes and bought a wide variety
of artefacts. A badly worded bribe
at someone's border cost him, but the tribe
had gorgeous boys… As always, he dined out
on local wits whose morals were in doubt.

But still, the object. *Ave atque vale*
the poet said, and published it, the way
his brother might have said *Cast a cold eye
on life, on death*, if able to reply.

On his return there were no souvenirs;
nor any that could check him at frontiers.

The Granite Poem

The granite poem
never breaks surface
pushing up
from underneath
makes tableland
The valleys grow
Generations
built their houses
out of the bones
of tableland
This is the house
that Jack built

The granite poem
is never published
Poets fossick
the stream gravel
people mine
the rich sills
that knock to be heard
ask to be polished
show their grain
on quarterly shelves
These are the poems
that Jack wrote

The granite poem:
cracked by frost
fragments weathered
years downriver
The parent rock
never changed shape
in anyone's life
Across the tableland
all those houses
those publications
a hundred Jacks
that granite built

Notes

'Attila': the poet Attila Jozsef's story is told briefly in Arthur Koestler's *The Invisible Writing*.

'Two Poems from *The Guide to Greece*': the comprehensive guidebook by Pausanias.

'The New Kenyans': The old man's memories are based on a conversation in C.G. Jung's *Memories, Dreams, Reflections*. Stanza 6 '...it's mere debugging...' refers to a paper 'The function of dream sleep', by F. Crick and G. Mitchison, *Nature*, 1983. Stanza 9 'Entirely mythic thoughts...' refers to the Areopagos, established by Athena to try the case of Orestes v. Furies; the supreme court of Greece still bears this name.

'Under the Volcano' is based on an account by John McPhee, originally published in *The New Yorker*, and reprinted in his collection *The Control of Nature*.

'Going to Visit the Grave': the Latin quotations are from Catullus's farewell to his brother, who was buried in Asia Minor.

www.ingramcontent.com/pod-product-compliance
Lightning Source LLC
Chambersburg PA
CBHW062153100526
44589CB00014B/1812